LUNA THE HOWLING HUSKY
FINDS HER HOWL

For the friends I met throughout my life that have loved me despite my quirks and oddities. You helped shape me and reign me in, but you also let me run free.

For the 2022-2023 first and second grade classes at Windsor Oaks Elementary School—your imagination, curiosity and love of books and learning reminded me of why I love what I do—and who I do it for.

Note to Families, Teachers & Counselors:

Luna's first solo book is a wonderful addition to the *Jake the Growling Dog* world. The story speaks to finding our voice and how one act of kindness can change someone's life for the better. A simple smile, a hello, or even giving them the space for silence can give a person that little something they need to turn a day or even a life around. We are more powerful than we know, and it's up to us to show our children how to use that power for good. Supplemental materials for this book include a seek-and-find, word search, conversation starter on ways to show kindness, and fun counting Luna's page.

Feel free to contact me with questions, to request supplemental materials, and for author readings.

Sending light and love to all!

Samantha

Luna the Howling Husky Finds Her Howl
Copyright © 2023 by Samantha Shannon

All rights reserved. Except as permitted under the U.S. Copyright Act of 1976, no part of this publication may be reproduced, distributed, or transmitted in any form or by any means, or stored in a database or retrieval system without the prior written permission of the publisher, except in the case of brief quotations embodied in critical articles and reviews.

Rawlings Books, LLC
Visit the world of Jake the Growling Dog and his friends at jakethegrowlingdog.com
Written and Created by Samantha Shannon
Illustrations by Lei Yang
Book Design by Lei Yang
Edited by Ariele Sieling & Melissa Stewart

The characters and events portrayed in this book are fictitious. Any similarity to real persons, living or dead, is coincidental and not intended by the author.

Paperback Edition ISBN: 978-1-7347447-8-1
eBook Edition ISBN: 978-1-7347447-9-8

LUNA THE HOWLING HUSKY

FINDS HER HOWL

Written by Samantha Shannon

Illustrated by Lei Yang

Rawlings Books, LLC

This adorable husky loves to chew and run.
Sleep's the only thing that ruins her fun.

She's happy and fluffy, but something bothers her each day.
Though her mind is made up, it doesn't come out the right way.

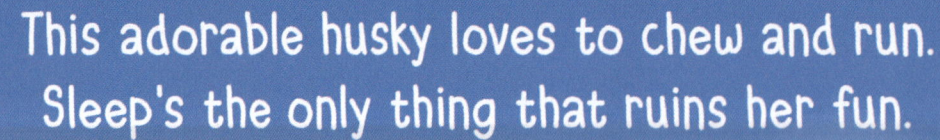

Luna can't howl at the sky like her brothers,
or *Ahh-wooooo* beautifully at the stars like her sisters.

She raises her furry chin but doesn't know why
only whimpers ring out each time she gives it a try.

Luna doesn't howl when the MOON is high,

and she doesn't howl when the GEESE honk by.

She can't howl when her siblings SING in unison,
Ahh-wooooo

and she can't howl songs about the WINTER wind.

No one knows why LUNA alone can't howl like the other huskies at HOME.

One winter day, when the snow was too cold to fall,
Luna wandered the yard trying to howl at a ball.

Many of her siblings had been adopted without any troubles,
scooped up in a blur of big eyes and warm snuggles.

But Luna has always been different, with brown eyes instead of blue, and a spidery blotch on her fur, sticky like morning dew.

The others played away from her, as she was too different from them. "What self-respecting husky can't howl?" she heard time and time again.

Today the ball was her friend, but it kept bopping away.
It wasn't a fan of her sad attempts; it only wanted to play.

"Today's the day," Luna told herself, snagging the ball in her teeth.
She tossed it up and caught it again, galloping off happily.

To Luna's surprise, the fluffy cat
dropped from the tree to the fence.
She was used to cats running away,
with a warning hiss that made her tense.

"Do you want to play? The others won't bother you while they're napping.
I guess howling makes them more tired." Luna's paw was nervously tapping.

The cat, whose name was Nemo, agreed to play chase in the yard.
Luna fumbled over her paws, and Nemo's short legs made going fast hard.

This kept the new friends close in speed and happily together at that.
The howlless dog and quiet cat enjoyed their merriment and chats.

They practiced *Mews* and *Ahh-wooooos*,
which soon changed from whimpers to laughs.
Neither of them finding much success
made it all seem less bad.

While lying in the grass beneath a tree, ears pricked up at the sound of puppies.
"Here they all come. I should go," Nemo said, getting up in a hurry.

"Yeah. Some of them won't know how to act," pouted Luna, now on her feet.
"But can we play again tomorrow? Same time—just you and me?"

Nemo agreed and lovingly rubbed her face along Luna's head.
Before she leapt over the fence, "You're a good friend," she said.

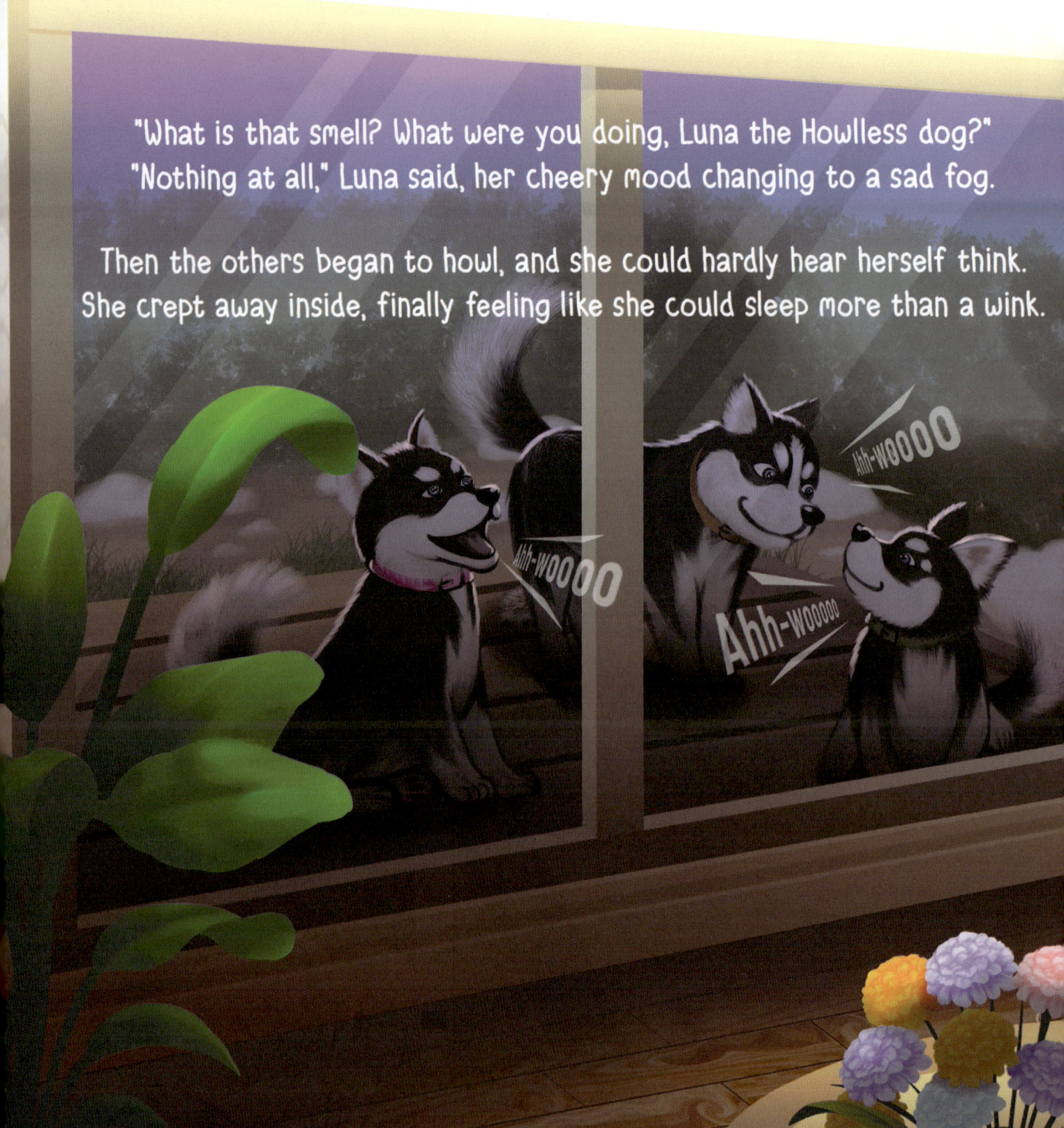

Luna awoke to fingers lifting her from her cozy bed.
Her tired eyes blinked open to a young girl petting her head.

"Momma, she's cute," the little girl cooed, giving Luna a squeeze.
"She's the perfect size to play with kitty. Can we adopt her? Please?"

"She is adorable," the child's mother replied.
"I thought I heard puppies here, but she's a sweet surprise.

How funny that your cat led you here. You'd think a cat would stay away."
"Not Nemo," the little girl chimed in. "She may be quiet, but she's so brave."

When Luna heard Nemo's name, she wriggled in the girl's lap.
She gave tickly sniffs into her hair and hands, making the child joyfully clap.

"Well, we have to take her," smiled the mom as her daughter giggled.
The two of them were already in love with the husky they both tickled.

Next came puppy kisses and zooming circles on silly paws.
Then something incredible happened when Luna heard her family's applause.

A joyful, magical sound took shape within Luna's tiny chest.
It filled her body with warmth and a dreamlike happiness.

Her first *Ahh-wooooo* was a beautiful sound that cascaded around the room. It felt like time stopped as the love between Luna and her new family began to bloom.

"See, momma, I told you her voice would be special, just like Nemo's. They will be the best of friends. I can't wait for them to say hello."

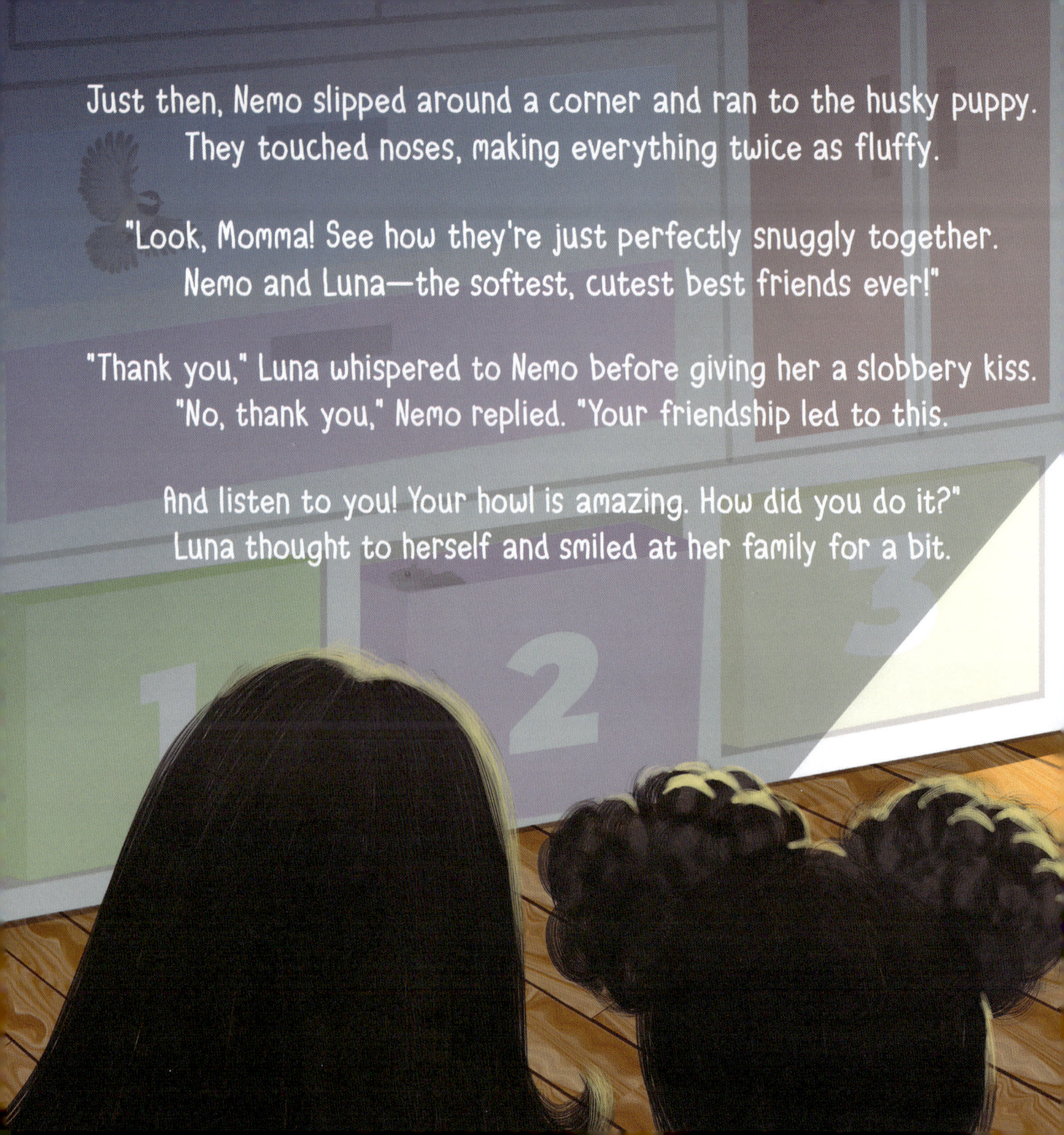

Just then, Nemo slipped around a corner and ran to the husky puppy.
They touched noses, making everything twice as fluffy.

"Look, Momma! See how they're just perfectly snuggly together.
Nemo and Luna—the softest, cutest best friends ever!"

"Thank you," Luna whispered to Nemo before giving her a slobbery kiss.
"No, thank you," Nemo replied. "Your friendship led to this.

And listen to you! Your howl is amazing. How did you do it?"
Luna thought to herself and smiled at her family for a bit.

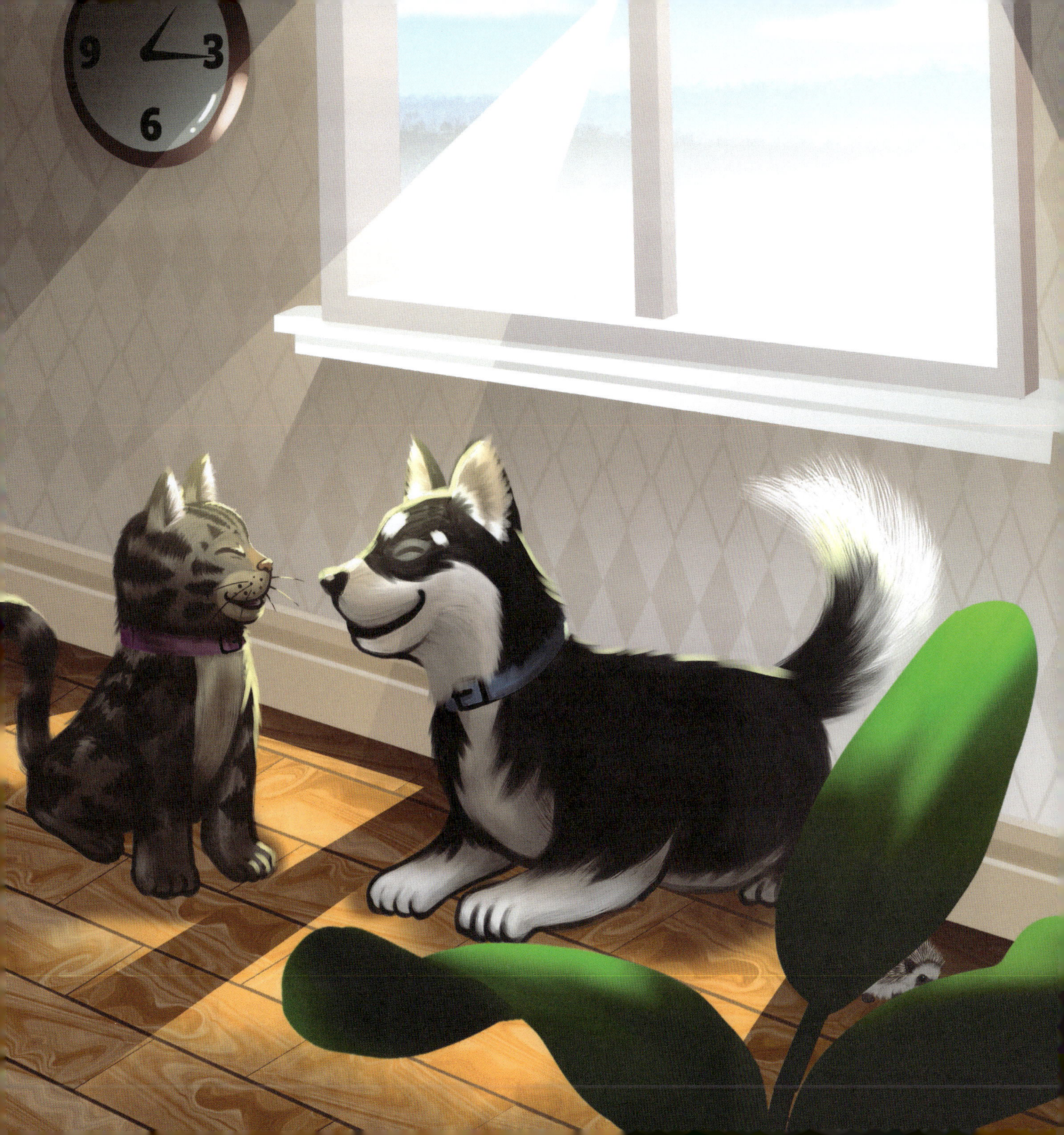
9
3
6

"Love," Luna answered, as the four of them snuggled close.
"The love of my new family canceled out the sadness and lows."

Luna and Nemo went home, and their friendship grew stronger each day.
A life where they accepted each other for who they are in every way.

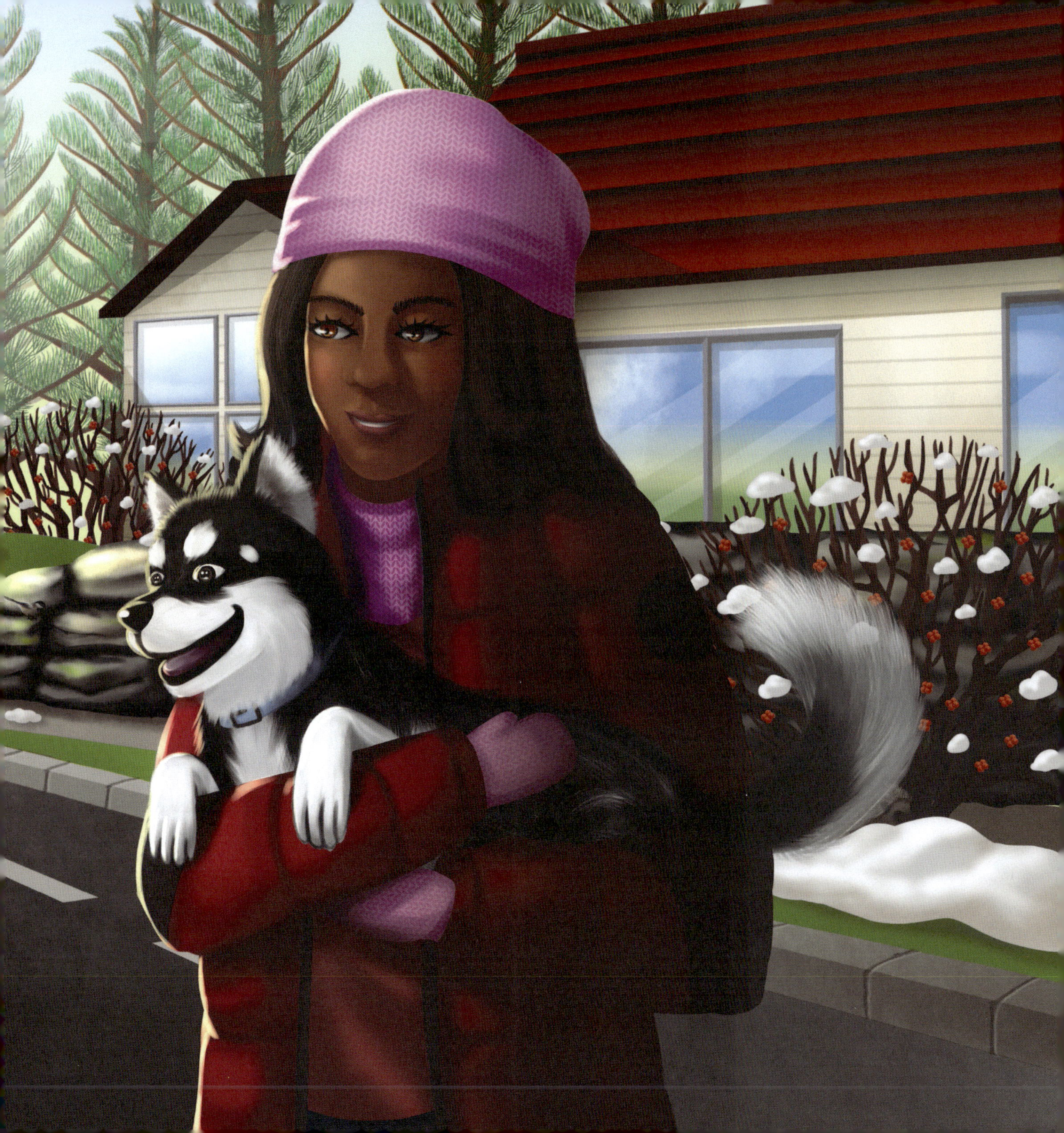

And now Luna howls when the MOON is high,

Ahh-wooooo

and she howls when the GEESE honk by.

HONK HONK HONK

Ahh-wooooo

She howls while NEMO whispers in unison,

Ahh-wooooo
MeOW

and she howls SONGS about her best friend.

Ahh-wooooo

She howls for the love of her FAMILY each day.
Howls of happiness that started when she asked a new friend to PLAY.

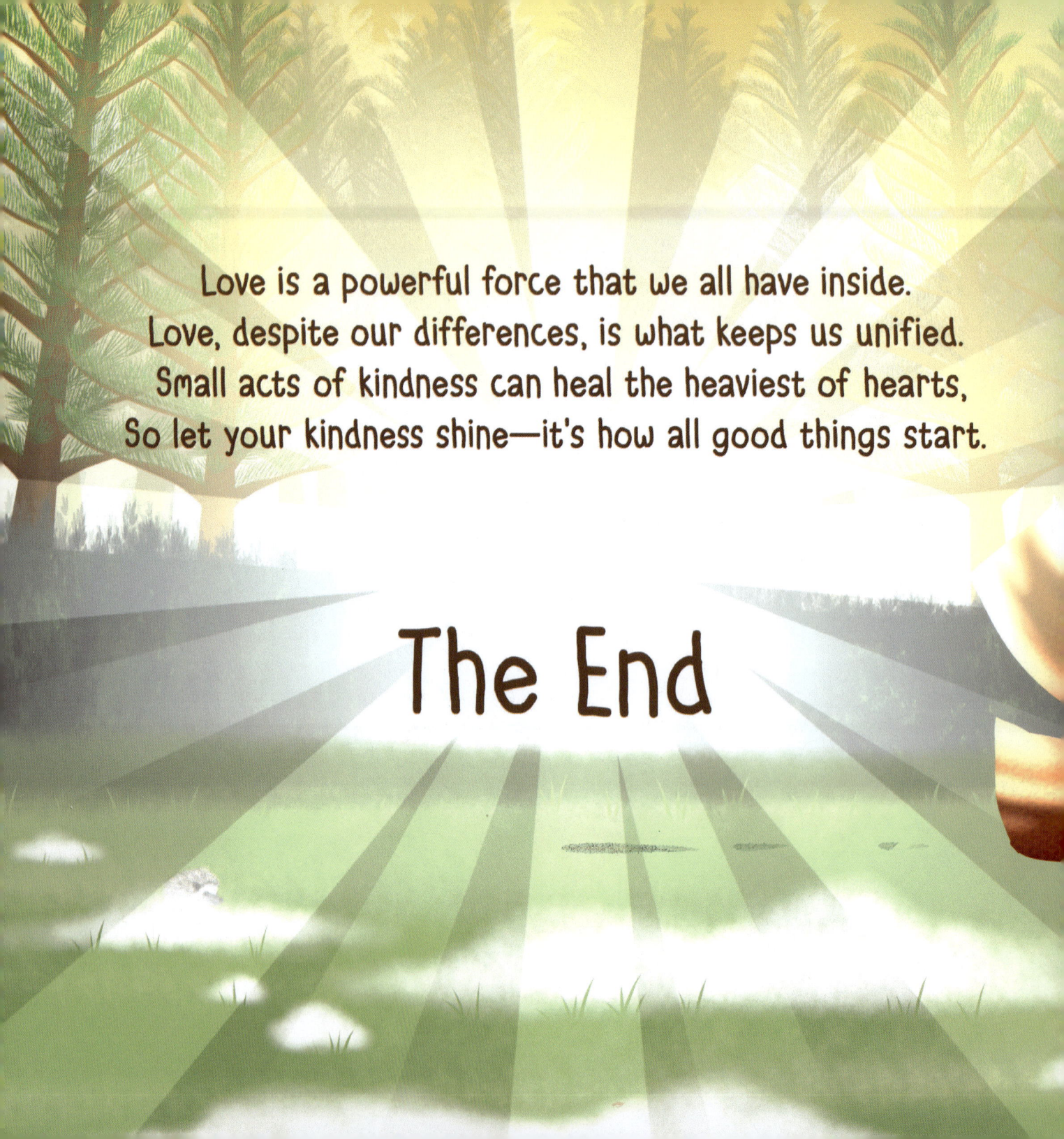

Love is a powerful force that we all have inside.
Love, despite our differences, is what keeps us unified.
Small acts of kindness can heal the heaviest of hearts,
So let your kindness shine—it's how all good things start.

The End

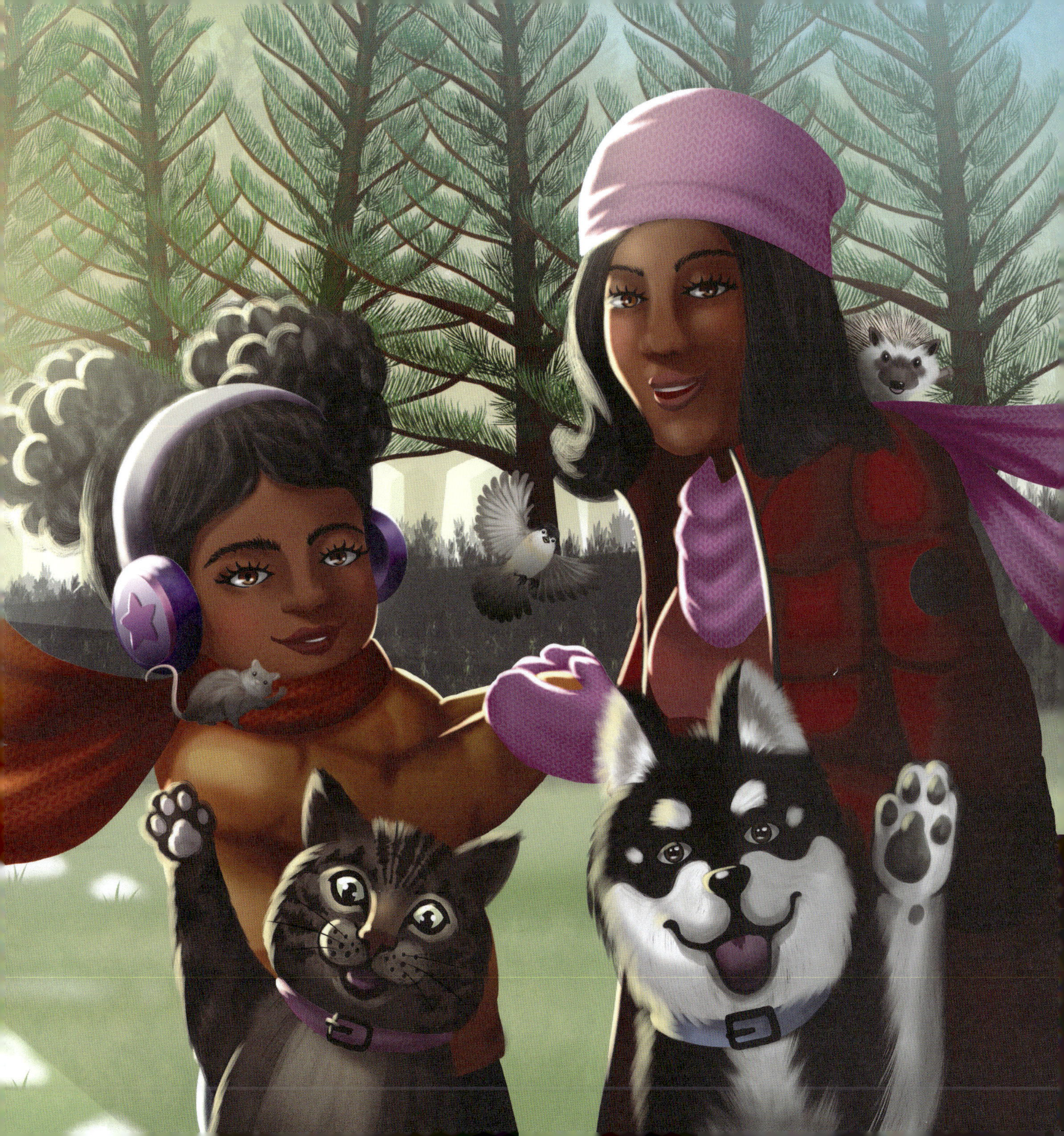

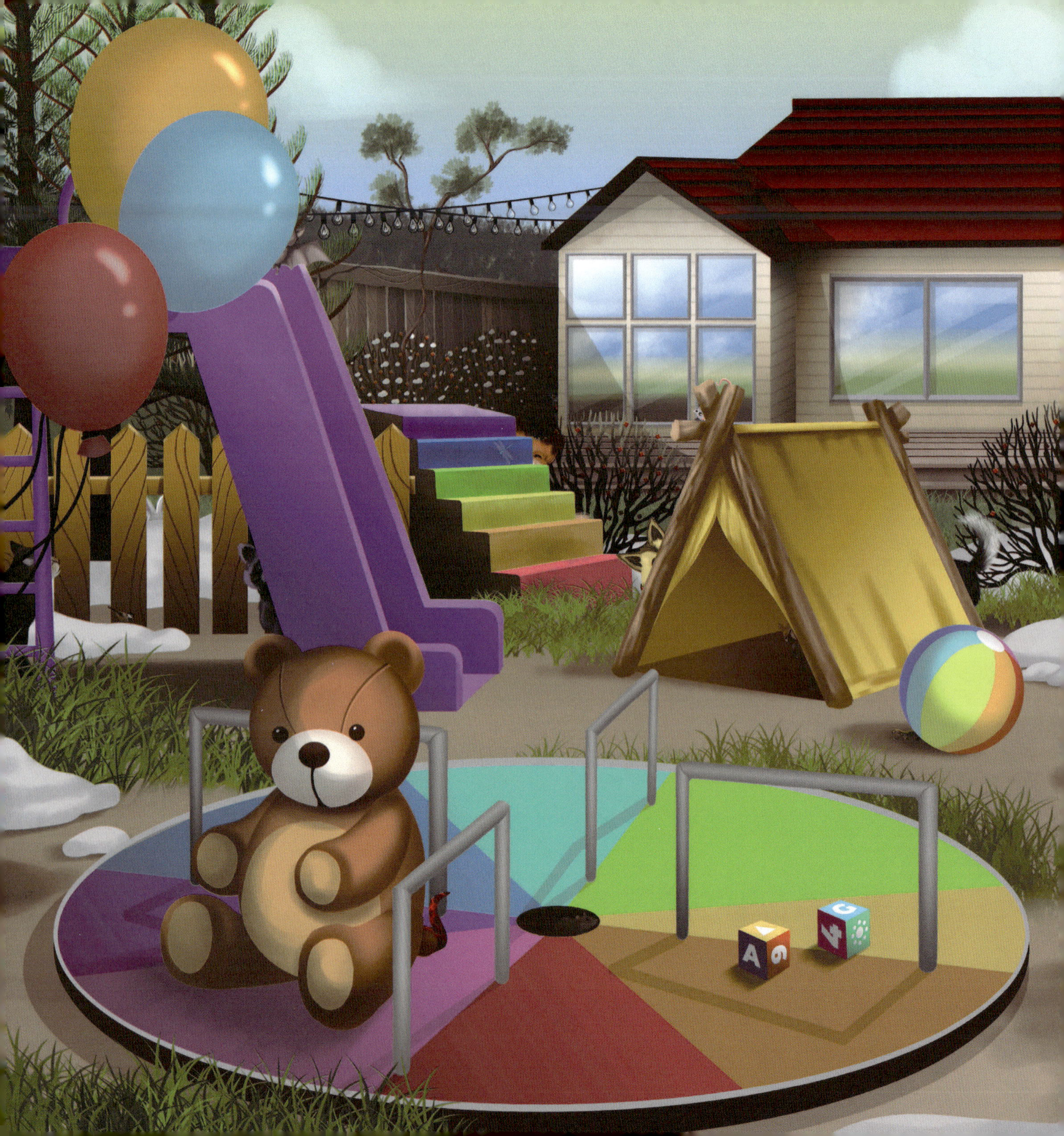

SEEK & FIND

HOW MANY LUNAS CAN YOU FIND

WORD SEARCH

C	B	M	K	H	A	F	L	G	H	S	K
D	N	I	F	U	Z	Z	Y	N	Z	I	I
F	J	P	R	S	E	R	V	I	D	L	N
A	R	S	I	K	N	M	J	Y	S	L	D
M	L	X	E	Y	U	O	C	A	T	Y	N
I	W	R	N	G	R	O	W	L	P	G	E
L	I	E	D	L	H	N	K	P	A	W	S
Y	U	P	S	B	X	L	U	T	C	R	S
N	T	S	H	A	P	P	I	N	E	S	S
J	A	I	I	L	U	N	A	E	U	H	B
K	B	H	P	L	Z	A	P	M	Q	Y	X
H	O	W	L	I	N	G	L	O	V	E	T

Cat Shy
Ball Luna
Love Moon
Snow Nemo
Paws Silly
Fuzzy Husky
Puppy
Family
Playing
Howling
Whisper
Kindness
Friendship
Happiness

Ways to Let Your Kindness Shine

By letting your kindness light shine, you can help others who may be hurting (just like Nemo and Luna did for each other). Check out Luna and Nemo's tips below, and let your light shine!

- Be there for a friend
- Share your smile
- Give genuine compliments
- Be friendly
- Show your creativity
- Show gratitude and positivity

Sometimes we make mistakes, and that's okay!

Everyone gets angry, frustrated, or sad. When we feel these emotions, we can sometimes be unkind to others. It happens to all of us, and that's okay. You can always show your kind self by apologizing to that person—and yourself too.

Standing up for yourself

This doesn't mean you can't stand up for yourself when someone isn't being kind to you or when you need to set your boundaries. You can stand up for yourself using a kind, direct voice to make your boundaries clear.

_____'s Kindness Page
(Child's name here)

(Directions: Fill in one of the shapes with ways you've been kind, who you've been kind to or who is kind to you! Read your kindness page over & add to it whenever you need a kindness boost!)

Critters

Did you find these cute critters on each page? They can be pretty tricky to find, but they also represent some important traits and themes.

Mouse
Kindness and Peace

Bird
Positive Change and Bravery

Hedgehog
Patience and Persistence

Meet the real Luna the Howling Husky and her friend Nemo!

READ MORE BOOKS BY

Samantha Shannon

Supporting the healthy socio-emotional development of all children with fun-loving & gentle tales of:

• Kindness • Sharing • Disability Awareness • Mindfulness • Diversity • Gratitude • Facing Fears • Stress Relief • Friendship • Grief • Loving-Kindness •

Jake and his friends love sharing their touching stories with everyone, and there's more to come!

jakethegrowlingdog.com

Printed in Great Britain
by Amazon